Self Publishing - The Secret Guide To Writing And Marketing A Best Seller

Adidas Wilson

Published by Adidas Wilson, 2017.

SELF PUBLISHING - THE SECRET GUIDE TO WRITING AND MARKETING A BEST SELLER

First edition. September 1, 2017.

Copyright © 2017 Adidas Wilson.

ISBN: 978-1393019909

Written by Adidas Wilson.

Table of Contents

Introduction

S elf-publishing is whereby an author publishes their book or any other media without involving an established publisher. If a book is physical, it is referred to as privately print. The author is in charge of every process including the design of the interior and cover, formats, distribution, public relations, price, and marketing. The author may decide to do all these by themselves or include companies that issue these services.

Self-publishing is not a new concept. The Joy of Cooking was self-published and printed in 1931. Fifty Shades of Grey, a best-seller by E.L James was also self-published due to public demand.

A while ago, authors had to spend a lot of money self-publishing since they had to purchase so many copies of their title and then find somewhere to store the inventory. Today, the ebook and print on demand technology enable authors to print a book or deliver it digitally when an order is placed.

Technology has brought a lot of improvement when it comes to books. Some of those advancements include;

• Online stores. Now readers can purchase books without physically visiting a bookstore.

• Tablet computers and e-book readers enable readers to have multiple books on a portable device.

• Anyone can access global distribution channels through online stores.

• The print-on demand technology produces high-quality products.

Every book should have an ISBN to uniquely identify its title—unless the author sells it directly to the public. It is advisable to obtain an ISBN and copyright rather than use one that belongs to a vanity press. Each book edition will require a separate ISBN.

Electronic (e-book) Publishing is the most popular among authors because the e-books can be created without upfront or per-book costs. There are also ebook formats and tools for creating electronic books. Some of the platforms that publish e-books include Smashwords, Pronoun, Amazon Kindle Direct Publishing, Blurb, and Papyrus Editor among others. Ebook formats include PDF, Mobi, Epub, etc.

Print on Demand includes printing high-quality books on order. Self-publishing authors consider this method to be economical, instead of printing so many books all at once. Blurb, Amazon, Createspace, Llumina Press and Lulu offer single books printing services at a fair cost—almost the same as the amount charged by publishing companies.

Publishing companies use to pay authors a fraction of the sales made from a book. Therefore, they only published books that were more likely to sell. It was tough for upcoming authors to get a contract. This led to the mushrooming of vanity publishers. They would publish any book, but the author had to pay upfront. Also, the author did not own the final book version and had no say in its distribution.

Self-publishing authors undertake all the activities surrounding the publishing. However, to be referred as self-published, the author does not necessarily have to do all the work by themselves. The author can decide to outsource some of the activities to companies or freelancers.

Chapter 1
How to Self-Publish

D o you have a great book idea but you do not know where to start? Or perhaps you have begun writing, and you would like to self-publish it, and you have no clue. Well, this book will give you a thorough understanding of all the processes involved in materializing your book. From writing to publishing and marketing it.

Before you even finish your rough draft you need to research extensively on your target market. Establish the genre of your book, whether nonfiction or fiction. Learn the market for that particular genre and your sub-genre (self-help, mystery, fantasy, and sci-fi). Familiarize yourself with the current trends in that subgenre so that you do not flood a saturated market. Look for what is missing and fill the gap. Take a look at existing books that are similar to yours and try to make yours a bit different.

BEFORE YOU CONSIDER anything else, you need to complete a rough draft of your book. You will need to put in hard work and discipline. It is advisable to set a schedule from the beginning and stick to it. Be patient as this process may take months or even years.

Try to look for advice from experienced authors even if it is online. In the end, the script may not be perfect but you will know what to do next.

Finding an editor is important if you want to create a great book. A professional editor will correct any mistakes in grammar or plot holes.

Use the criticism to make your book even better. You can get an experienced content and copy editor on most of the reputable freelancing sites online.

This is where you utilize all the correction and criticism you got from fast checkers, readers, and your editor. Aim at creating a perfect final draft.

You cannot do everything alone. You may be a great author, but you are not a good editor or designer. Create a team of professionals to help you come up with an excellent book.

When you have reviews, the chances of your book selling are higher than when you do not. Find reviewers in the genre you are writing about. Usually, the reviews will appear on the back cover of your book and maybe on retailers' websites.

For a reader to pick your book from the shelf, the cover has to be compelling. Find an expert designer to create a cover for you. A great cover should convey the content of the book and convince the reader to pick it.

8. Retail

This involves publishing the final copy to start selling. You can choose between self-publishing and a traditional publisher. If you opt to self-publish, do not overlook design and distribution. Give these two aspects enough consideration.

9. Promotion, Marketing, and Distribution

Having your book in the market is one thing; ensuring that it sells is another. One secret to selling your book is to have it ordered by a leading distributor like Amazon. You can hire a professional marketer to market your book and also promote you as an author.

10. Keep Going

The whole process of writing and publishing a book may be cumbersome but never give up. Keep going.

Having your book out in the market and selling is not easy, but it is doable. Be determined and go through the above steps thoroughly.

Do everything right and enjoy the process, the next best seller might be yours.

Chapter 2

Guest blogging to Promote Your Book

GUEST BLOGGING IS huge right now and not only can it be a great way of promoting your book but a free way too, here's six advantages that guest blogging can have for authors:

1) Amplify your reputation in your field – When your prospective audience see your name on popular sites it shows you're experienced in your niche as well as giving you a chance to showcase your talents.

2) Grow your audience – If you're posting a guest post on a popular site that is in your niche, the sites large and engaged audiences are all becoming your prospective audience as well. If they like what they read they're likely to look out for things you write in the future.

3) Increase your sales – This one is obviously a big deal, if you're trying to promote the sale of your book then every guest post you write can be a chance of including a direct link to purchase your book.

4) Get reviews without begging – If you can contact a popular blogger and offer to write a guest post from them, they're a lot more likely to get back to you and review your blog when you ask them. You're offering them something valuable instead of asking for a favour. You get your book promoted and reviewed, and they get new content for their website.

5) Build your subscriber list – Guest blogging is a useful tool in getting new subscribers and helping you build up your email list. As I mentioned earlier if the audience like what you write they will read more of your work and are much more likely to subscribe. Guest blogging on a few different popular sites would give you an opportunity to gain entire audiences in your niche topic at once.

6) Plan a virtual book tour – If you plan a guest post campaign it can increase your sales throughout a book launch.

IF IT SOUNDS LIKE GUEST blogging is for you then keep reading for 6 steps to start guest blogging,

1) Research potential blogs to guest post – You need to find popular blogs in your niche that have the type of audience you're aiming for.

2) What post ideas have you got? – You need to come up with a few post ideas or sample headlines (try thinking of 3 to 5 ideas for each blog you're targeting). It's good to look at recent blog posts that have been popular and don't use the same ideas but take the topics from fresh angles.

3) Send your pitches – Look for any writers guidelines to follow on their sites and use their blog contact form or email

the blogger. Write your pitch to suite the blog you're targeting and include your proposed blog post topics.

4) Make sure your guest post is top-quality – When you get accepted you need to show other potential target sites that you can do a good job, and you need to catch the audience's attention. You shouldn't re-use content from your own blog write something fresh and unless required by blogger make sure it's over 1000 words. Write your author byline at the bottom of the page and include your Amazon book page link if it fits with your topic.

5) Respond – When your guest blog post is published, always respond to the comments. You can also share the post to social media and send it to your subscribers in your email list.

6) Follow up – If your first guest post goes well then keep going. Follow up on guest posts you do that seem to increase your sales or subscribers and ask for more opportunities to write a guest post, build a relationship with the bloggers and even become a regular contributor if you can.

Chapter 3

A Guide to Amazon Book Reviews

Most authors love Amazon reviews. Amazon is a major books' distributor, and new self-published books have the chance of being reviewed alongside best sellers. Amazon reviews can validate your book and make you famous (or otherwise). Good reviews will drive more buyers to your book; so if you are skeptical about Amazon reviews, don't be.

Many people do not understand how Amazon reviews are handled and this has caused a lot of confusion. Amazon is a big player in the game, and almost every author aims at having positive reviews. Therefore, Amazon has strict regulations to make the reviews as truthful as possible.

Amazon began pulling down nepotistic reviews in 2012, and to some authors, this seemed unfair. Moreover, it is not clear what will cause a perceived nepotistic review to be removed. Therefore, the best thing is for reviewers to be honest. If a reviewer has a relationship with an author, they should say it in the review. Amazon seems to appreciate the transparency and such reviews stand.

In as much as Amazon has strict rules and guidelines in place, sometimes enforcement of those rules may seem inconsistent. For example, if a smear campaign is launched against a particular author, Amazon may delete some of the ugly comments and leave others. If you feel directly attacked in any way, it would be best to appeal directly to Amazon in a polite way and be consistent.

• Never get into an argument with a reviewer in the review section. Do not directly defend your book or yourself. In the case of a negative review, just answer "no" to the question that reads, "Was this review helpful to you?"

• Amazon only legitimizes reviews from verified buyers. However, to be a verified buyer you do not have to buy the book from Amazon. You just have to be honest on where you purchased the book and admit if you got it for free. Some writers get so many reviews from readers who got the book for free.

• Never shy away from asking for reviews, especially when someone sends a positive note about your book. Also, if you know great reviewers email them and ask them to review your book on Amazon.

• Amazon reviews are ideal for marketing, especially if you have a significant number of reviews. While promoting your book, you can include something like, "My book has 75 Amazon reviews. "Always quote great reviews in your marketing platforms and websites.

For now, there is no question that Amazon is king when it comes to reviews. It is the platform on which authors carefully track their book's success, and it is where readers go when they need great books. Even so, it is not the only place to help you succeed. Of course, reviews are great, but you need to supplement them with other forms of promotion. One last tip, always have multiple buying options for potential readers when you are marketing your book.

Chapter 4

How Indie Authors Can Create Super fans

F inding readers is one thing, but creating a relationship with them is another. So many blogs and marketers will advise you on how to find readers, but very few will give you advice on how you care for them. With a few adjustments to your publishing process, you have a chance to uncover super fans who are passionate readers.

Super fans are a crucial part of your writing experience. They spread the word about your work and buy all of your books. They will always be there to preorder the next book from you and give it an excellent review.

Attracting super fans can take minutes, months or even years. Before you begin to build the ideal environment for super fans, you need to get in their minds and desire to know why they read. It could be for knowledge, pleasure or both.

Anytime you interact with your readers; whether it is at a conference, on social media, or when they are reading your book, they get an insight of who you are. Through these interactions, you may earn their confidence, trust, and admiration or lose it.

Readers tend to protect their limited resources of money, attention and time. Readers' minds, both subconscious and conscious are modeled to notice negative and positive inputs and store them on some virtual mental scorecards. These scorecards influence the reader's decisions every passing second. So every high-risk, repulsive or unsatisfying piece of work is abandoned or ignored. Therefore, readers will always be inclined towards authors who can satisfy their desires.

The scores kept in the scorecards are cumulative—meaning that three typos in the entire book may not chase a reader away but typos on each page could. And that will tarnish your name as an author.

Below are crucial areas that could make you uncover super fans or chase readers away for good.

1. Cover Design

A great cover promises the reader something. It will either convince the reader that the book is what they need or blow them off. Invest in design, symbolism, and imagery by hiring professionals. Most readers do not take homemade covers seriously, but a professionally created cover is appealing and promising.

2. Book Description

Your description is very crucial. Those are the first words that a potential reader will read. Most self-published books have the worst book descriptions—characterized by poor sentence casing, typos, and inadequate information. When a reader notices this sloppiness, they get the idea that the book is not worth their time.

3. Author persona

The way you market yourself as an author gives readers an impression of who you are. Carve the best image of yourself both online and offline

4. Formatting And design

Your e-books should have a neat, organized and attractive design. From the font sizes to the paragraph construction, ensure everything is flawless and clean.

5. Writing

Make your book interesting, let it be a page-turner. With every page, stimulate, tease and hook your readers.

6. Improved Back Matter

At the end of the book, most authors do not add anything. For them, end of story means end of story. It is always nice to add sections like About the Author, Other Books by This Author and Connect with the Author.

Do not always aim at getting new readers; ensure that you keep the ones that you have. They make part of your marketing team in a way.

Chapter 5

How to Market Your Book

In your lifetime you will hear someone say they have hundreds of copies of their masterpiece just lying somewhere in the house. They will go on and on about how they could become a millionaire if only they could sell the copies. You do not want to be that "someone"—and if you don't, you have to market your book seriously.

Most self-published writers won't know much pertaining to sales and business. Marketing, unlike writing, requires the author to go out and communicate with potential readers; so that your book can be out there for everyone to see it.

Many self-publishers increase their chances of success by thinking about marketing before they write a book. It is important to identify the reason for writing the book and its benefit to your readers. Knowing who your target market is and what they read, will give you a clear goal for writing the book and a clear marketing strategy.

MOST AUTHORS PREFER this method of marketing. The main reason being that readers trust book reviews; they are honest, editorial and not promotional. A majority of readers usually read the reviews before they purchase a book. Aim at getting high honest reviews for your book.

It is difficult for self-publishers to predict the level of marketing effort they have to put in to make their books sell. Amazingly, the internet offers a level platform where even upcoming publishers can compete with established publishing companies.

It is not easy; you will have to make an effort. However, it is something you cannot afford to relinquish. Online marketing is much cheaper and if utilized correctly, more productive than the traditional marketing methods.

To get the most out of online marketing; ensure that you have your author platform and effectively use of social media to market yourself.

THERE IS NO DEFINITE answer to getting your book on the bestseller list; otherwise, every writer would be at the top. A wise thing would be to learn from other writers' experiences. Look for interviews and know what to do and what to avoid.

Always consider book marketing a business. Creating the ultimate marketing skills requires you to define your reason for writing and your target audience. You will then know how to communicate with potential readers effectively. You may find your success by marketing on social media, putting your book on a bookstore shelf, using online traffic keywords, or even peddling your book in presentations and conventions.

You can only discover your success by figuring out the perfect way to communicate to your readers. What worked for another author might not work for you. Put yourself in your readers' minds, think like them, and you will know what they want and how you can reach them. Do not end up with piles of your manuscripts lying somewhere gathering dust.

Chapter 6
Tips to Creating Best Selling Book Ideas

Almost everyone can write a book. However, not everyone can write a bestseller. You may write a book to follow your passion or realize a dream but in the end you want your book to sell. Every author would appreciate a high rank on Amazon.

Search Engine Optimization (SEO)

Some people write books based on keywords. Whether you are passionate about writing or not, focusing on saleable terms can get you on top of Google's page. Maybe this is not how you want to write your book, but it has its advantages. If you choose to go with SEO consider the following;

• You do not have to deviate from your original book plan, but you will have to adjust it to fit in the trending search or topic. If you write it according to popular topics, keep in mind that speed is of the essence.

• Use keywords in the book title and subtitle to increase your exposure in search.

Make your topic narrower. Do not focus on a vast topic. For example, if you want to write a book about selling or buying your first home, narrow down on specific subjects in the industry and write a series of books. You can write about; buying your first home for singles, buying your first home for with a domestic partner and so forth.

The idea is to choose a specialized topic that solves a particular problem—consumers like that. The books do not even have to be long. Also, authors with multiple titles tend to do better on Amazon.

When you have identified the keywords in your target market,

• Go to Kindle Store tab on Amazon and type in "selling book".

• Click on any of the suggestions (best-selling books in Kindle Store, top selling books on Kindle Store etc.)

• Take a good look at the books that will come up then click on the "customers also bought" option.

Target books with a low sales rank, about 20,000.

Keeping It Short and Narrow

Long books will always be there, but there is a high demand for shorter, niche books that focus on a specific subject. Do not stop writing long books all together. For a short book, 10,000 to 17,000 words are acceptable—avoid filler and fluff words, be clear and precise.

Other Methods for Developing Book Ideas

A lot of research is applied when writing a book; especially on the book topic and content. In addition, take a look at existing books that are similar to yours in the market. Read their reviews. The negative ones will help you know what is missing and what is needed.

Creating a bestselling book idea is not as complicated as it may sound. It basically entails research just like you have been doing. Only now you will research with a specific goal—to find keywords and trending topics. Remember to keep it short and narrow, writing a series of short and precise books. Nonetheless, be careful not to write a very short book that readers see almost all of it in the "look inside the book" feature on Amazon. They will just window shop and not buy it eventually.

Chapter 7
Email List

Many successful authors agree that an email list is a must-have for every author—regardless of your genre. But it is not just important because great authors agree; here are five more reasons.

Obviously, the difference between a best-selling author and a writer who is barely making it is the audience size. Some authors launch their books successfully by just sending a "click here to buy my book" email and the sales move forward overnight. Yes, it happens.

You cannot sell your book if you have no one to listen to you and buy from you. When you have your audience (email list), you get both of those things.

A majority of authors think that just because they have a large following on social media, they do not need a list. But look at it this way, that social media platform does not belong to you; Facebook, Twitter, YouTube etc., are the ones that own the audience. Facebook may suspend your page or Twitter may block your account, and then what?

Social media is great, and you can generate a lot of traffic, but it is wise to create an email list from there.

The main reason for building an email list is so that you can get noticed. You want people to click your link every time you send it out, whether it is a link to your blog or book promotion. However, if you have, 15000 followers on Twitter, and you send out a link you may get just a hundred clicks. On the other hand, if you have an email list of 4000 and you send out a link you may get 1000.

There is too much content on social media and people may not even see your link.

Your email list will build your audience, but that is not all. You create a relationship with your audience and get them to trust you even more. When someone gives you their email address, it shows that they trust you to deliver quality content and not spam them.

After you create the email list, follow up regularly and engage with your audience. Also, get a tailored auto-responder to make it convenient for you and the audience.

How great is it that you can now promote your book without paying extra cash? Just send your list a link asking them to buy your book. Nonetheless, your list is more than just an audience. Your list is part of your marketing team somehow. They will happily and freely spread the word about your work. Also, authors with their own audience command more respect. You can even ask your audience what you should write about next and get information on hot topics.

Building your email list is neither complicated nor too expensive. Some email service providers like Mailchimp are free. With a sizeable list, you are assured of sales, a personalized audience and even a small marketing team. Sign up today and begin to enjoy the benefits.

Chapter 8
Book Landing Page

There are so many mistakes that authors make while selling books on Amazon, and one of them is promoting their Amazon book sales page. If you are looking to make more sales and have more people on your email list, then do not market your Amazon book sales page.

Of course, you will have to set up a sales page on Amazon if you want to sell through the site. And you will have to optimize it to drive more sales.

To promote it successfully and sell your book online you need conversation and attention; convert internet surfers into your website visitors and make them buy your book.

If you go on advertising your Amazon sales page, the truth is that most people will visit the site and not buy the book, worse still, they may never return to the site. Also, you will never know who visited and left your site.

Before today's consumers can buy a book, they need to be informed and assured—something that cannot happen with one site visit. The solution is to send potential buyers to your landing page first instead of Amazon.

A website is like a standalone web page. The page is designed for a particular purpose and a visitor can "land" on it. Its primary objective is to generate more leads and sales. Also, it is easier to make, unlike a website.

One advantage of a landing page is that it has buying options for a visitor who would like to buy your book immediately and in case they do not buy; their information is captured to enable future follow-ups.

The top part of the page is a precious portion, use it wisely. If users do not scroll down, this is your only chance to convince them. You can just add an Obvious Opt-In Panel with three critical sections;

- A catchy message
- A call-to-action—encouragement to participate on your website
- An opt-in form to get their email address and add to your email list

THE NEXT SECTION IS where you introduce your book. It may be great, but people always want to know what's in it for them. Let your introduction be centered on the reader; how the book is perfect for them or how it will impact their lives.

Social proof is social influence whereby a person's actions affect another person's choice. With so many books in the market, people rely on social proofs to decide what book to buy. Use social proofs wisely. Some types of social proofs include; celebrity endorsements, reviews and testimonials.

Unlike selling on Amazon, while selling on your landing page, you can sell at a fair price. You can have three separate packages for the same book without restrictions.

A landing page is a must-have for any author, and so is an email list. Nothing compares to having your audience and having a relationship with them. Make a point of creating those two today.

Chapter 9

Write a Nonfiction EBook

Writing an average-length non-fiction book is no easy task, much less writing a great one. You will need to be a conversationalist, psychologist, observer, talented weaver of words and poet— all at the same time. A lot of skill and discipline is required. The following tips are tried and proven; they will guide you on how to write a book that readers cannot resist.

1. Know Your Target audience

Not everybody is your audience. You have to narrow down and focus on a particular person and know how to make them happy. You cannot target everybody since people have different tastes and preferences. If you narrow down to a precise audience, the chances of your book being successful are higher.

2. Know Your Competition

Most probably, your eBook idea is not unique. Similar books will always be there. Present your book in a relatable and understandable way, use your unique voice. Find the gaps that have been left by the eBook's in your niche and fill them. A niche may seem overcrowded, but you have a chance if you present your eBook nicely. Moreover, too many books in a particular niche mean that it is a "hot" industry.

3. Try Real Life Examples

Readers love a book that relates to them. Use examples of people who applied your advice and succeeded and examples of people who failed at certain things and even your life examples. Let them learn from you and your experiences.

4. Read More Than You Write

Reading should be one of the biggest parts of an author's life. Read to get inspiration, to research and to study your competition. Buy books similar to yours (especially those that have been recently published); this will help you fill in the gaps they have left. Read to learn about various writing styles and improve yours at the same time. Go online and read about what people think about your topic.

5. Monitor Your Market

You need to observe your market. What are they saying about the books in your niche? Maybe the books being released are all giving the same old information. Maybe they need new content or a unique perspective. Visit Amazon and read reviews of the books in your niche. Use the negative reviews to help you give the readers what they want.

6. Be Courageous With What You Do Not Know

It is nice to write about what you are familiar with. However, once in a while venture out of your comfort zone. If you decide to write about something you are not entirely comfortable with, it is okay to ask potential readers for advice and experience.

7. Make Use of Humor

No matter how dull or dry your content is, humor will always make it relatable to your audience. It will make the boring parts livelier, relieve tension and make your readers happy.

The above tips are a sure way to write a great book that readers will love. Always have a specific audience and aim at satisfying them. Read as much as you can about everything; you can never have too much knowledge. Have courage getting out of your comfort zone and finally, never underestimate the power of a joke.

Chapter 10

How Long Should Your EBook Be?

A good book is never long, and a bad book is never short. This applies to both eBook and print books. The question is, "what is the correct length for your eBook?" Before you determine the perfect length for your book, there are some factors you need to consider.

When turning your eBook into a print book, you will have to consider the length. Page restrictions apply when it comes to print books. A very thin book can barely be noticed when placed on the shelf with larger ones.

Even when writing an eBook, length is critical. Most eBook's in the market are short, and some experts believe that readers love short books. On the other hand, some experts say that longer eBooks sell more.

Most non-fiction books range from 50,000 to 70,000 words while biographies go up to 200,000 words. Self-help books (how-tos) are usually short with an average of 40,000 words. As you can see, it is like every category has an average length. Try to compare successful books in your category to determine the optimum length for your book.

Every book should be long enough to share all the information it was meant to. Let your book be as long or as short as it has to be. Share the knowledge or tell your story in the necessary amount of words; no more, no less. After all, you are a self-publisher.

When you decide to publish your book traditionally, you will always plan and agree with your publisher on the page count, expenses, profit-and-loss statement, design, etc. However, after writing and reviewing your book, the words could be far more than you agreed.

If there is no way you can squeeze the text, you will end up slashing significant content.

EBooks do not have these restrictions, and design is not important unless you are planning to have a print version later on.

Estimating your page and word count helps you to gauge the cost of production beforehand. A longer book will cost you more when you produce it, and this means it has to sell more for you to make a profit.

IT IS NOT ADVISABLE to jump into writing a book without a clear plan. Before you start, ensure that;
- You have table of contents
- You write chapter summaries
- You assess the length of similar existing books
- You have the desired length for your book
- You have an idea how long each chapter should be

All these guidelines will enable you to remain on track without writing unnecessary words. Since every book should be as long as it needs to be, having an idea and a plan helps you to write exactly what you need to. You will work smart and not hard. In the end, you will have a great book that might be at the top of the charts.

Chapter 11

Finding a Niche as a Self-Publisher

Finding a profitable niche is no easy task for any aspiring self-publisher. Many new authors think they can just write a book about anything and they will make money. Too bad this is never the case.

If you are looking to make money from your book, you have to tap into potential readers' interest. Find out what people would like to read. What information or answers are they actively seeking? You may write a great book, but if nobody is interested in the topic, it will not sell.

The advantage of writing something you are passionate about is that you are likely to write a great book since you are interested in the topic and you are conversant with it. However, the downside of this tactic is the subject may not appeal to readers and it ends up not selling. If no one likes the topic, it doesn't matter how good the book is or how much effort you will put in marketing it.

If you publish a book on a topic that is in demand, its chances of success will be high, and the launch is very likely to be a success. Take your time and find out what books are selling well. Know what the readers want, what they are looking for and what they are interested in. You are likely to get a profitable niche this way.

1. Find Best Selling Lists

Visit sites like Amazon, Barnes & Noble, or even just Google and search for best selling lists. Go through the lists and try to find a pattern or correlation. If you find a certain topic dominating in the top one hundred, for example, diets and weight loss, then you know that people are interested in that niche.

It is wise to narrow it down further to a specific category or a specific book. Amazon lets you look at how well (or not) individual books are selling and they rank the books. So you will know what might sell and what might not.

2. Go to Bookstores

Not many people try this, yet it yields results. Bookstores will always place their best sellers at the front. See if there are similar topics on display. Going to a bookstore will also help you choose a topic because you can copy one.

Another tip is to hang out at the store and see what book attracts people's attention and what section most people frequently visit.

3. Go on Viral News and Media Sites

These viral news sites often post articles about almost everything. By visiting them, you can see what topics get the most reads and clicks. If people read about social media marketing, then probably it is a subject they are willing to spend money on. They will appreciate a great book on that particular topic.

These are the main ways to find readers' interests. Visit book retailing sites and see what is selling the most or go to bookstores and see for yourself what people are most interested in. Finally, you can visit viral news sites and get the hottest topic. You will have an idea of the topics that are likely to sell and those that are likely to be a total fail.

Chapter 12

Marketing Video for your Book

It is shocking that in this era where technology has taken over, some people do not know what kind of videos they can create. There are numerous ways of doing a video, and you are only allowing your imagination to limit you.

Let this list guide you in creating the perfect marketing video. However, remember that in video marketing, just as in everything, your goals should determine your direction. A particular type of video may be useful for one goal but ineffective for another.

1. Talking Head

This is probably the most common type, the head and shoulders direct to the camera. It works better for personal promotional purposes; direct appeals, "first impression" videos, and "about me "videos on your website.

2. Interview

This is similar to talking head but with one additional person making it an interview video. The interview video can comprise of more than two people. Alternatively, it can be "news style" whereby the interviewer is off camera, and the interviewee is on camera.

3. Live Webcast

Live streaming is becoming more popular every day. It allows you to interact with viewers in real time. With an idea and a webcam, you can easily to create your webcast.

4. Video PowerPoint

Narrated PowerPoint is popular because it is simple. Anyone with PowerPoint (or Keynote for Mac) can add their narration and have their video.

5. Video Tips Series

The Video Tips Series is perfect if you are looking to establish a presence on YouTube. They help you improve your SEO and credibility in addition to making you look like an expert.

6. Live Demo (on-camera)

On camera, demonstrations are very effective. Some people prefer to teach live, and others like to use a whiteboard. Jing is great for brief videos as it is fast, flexible and free.

7. Recorded Demo/Screencast

Instead of going live, you can record your demo from your computer screen. Screencast videos are quite popular so you should consider having them when doing marketing videos.

8. Photo Montage

Websites such as OneTrueMedia.com, Animoto.com and Stupeflix.com make it so easy to create a photo/video montage just by dragging and dropping.

9. Sales Video

Technically any video can be a sales video, but this refers to a sales page that comprises entirely of a video and a "buy" button. The videos are usually a text and narration.

10. Launch Series

Launch series videos come before a sales video. They are released in a series of three or four. Their main aim is to launch a product or do a major promotion.

11. Video Testimonials

They are useful for providing social proof. Make a habit of collecting video testimonials and include them in your website or sales page.

Other types of videos include;

12. Product Videos

13. Teaching/Webinar Video
14. Animated Video
15. Sizzle Reel
16. Video Email

With these types of videos and many others, you can never run out of options. Create a video that suits your audience and market your product in the most efficient manner.

Chapter 13

Mistakes Self-Publishers make on Book Covers

Many self-published authors do not take cover designs seriously, and they make terrible ones that end up on Kindle Cover Disasters or Lousy Book Covers lists.

Sometimes, your book does not sell because the cover is poorly designed. Check the following four common mistakes to avoid making a lousy cover—if you have not made one already.

Your book cover must never look self-published—ever. To be honest, most homemade covers look bad because the authors have no sense of design and they always disregard the rules of making great covers.

There is nothing wrong with someone making their cover. Self-publishing does not mean operating on a minimum budget and low quality. But most readers will never get that. They will always consider self-published books to be of low quality—produced by amateurs without quality control. They think self-published authors are too poor to be picked by mainstream publishers.

Therefore, if you are self-publishing, invest in a good cover design. Let it reflect professionalism and high quality.

Creating a book cover calls for creativity and many people like to be unique when being creative—which is good. However, you do not have to be too unique. Do not create a design that has never been seen in the market before.

All books in a genre follow a particular pattern. If you are writing a cookbook ensure that it looks like the other cookbooks in the market. Your cover should capture a reader's attention by looking attractive, not out of place. Picture your book displayed with other books of the same genre, does it look like it belongs there?

The fear of missing out is common across all humans. Sometimes, this fear influences authors when they are designing their covers. You must have seen at least one of those books with so many things on them.

Most of those authors think that they have to reveal all the contents of the book through the cover. Letting your cover convey the book content is good but how about just hinting instead of exposing everything? Too much information on the cover might confuse your audience and turn them away.

You have probably come across book covers that look so busy and messy—no hierarchy. It looks like a confusion of texts and pictures. It is like mistake number three above but on another level. Everything on the cover (the text, images and color) is screaming to catch your attention. You cannot even see what the book is about and you lose interest very fast.

You may be an outstanding author, but if your cover does not appeal to readers they will not pick it up, and all your efforts will be in vain. If you made any of the mistakes above, consider a makeover. Invest in a professional designer and get your book to sell.

Chapter 14
Why Self-Published Books Don't Sell

"Why won't my book sell?" This is probably the most asked question by self-publishers. Sometimes, the reasons are so obvious; take a glance at their books, you can name several.

Some friends and relatives may buy your book to show their support, but one bad Amazon review from a reader will dampen your overall sales. Again, you might convince a few people to give your book five-star reviews on Amazon, however, too many five-star reviews coupled with one and two-star reviews will reveal the book is poorly edited. Get a professional editor to edit your book and get rid of any errors.

Easy-to-read, professional and neat covers sell more than poorly done covers. Readers can always tell a cheap, horrible cover when they see one. Great covers attract readers while poor covers will result in poor sales. If you cannot make an appealing book cover, invest in a book cover designer

Some books are just poorly written. They have nothing to offer except sales letter after sales letter, trying to convince you to buy this or that. There is nothing wrong with having affiliate links in your books but at least let your content outweigh your advertisements.

Books in a popular niche will always do well. Visit Amazon and if you see 600 books in your niche, you are on the right track. When books show hundreds in that category, it does not mean that niche is oversaturated; it only means that niche is "hot".

Book layout software is there for a reason. You cannot use Ms Word to format your book—readers will tell it is cheaply self-published from miles away. Money is hard to come by and no reader wants to waste any of it on a cheaply designed book.

FORMATTING IS CRITICAL when it comes to eBooks. Words appearing randomly, bad spacing, graphics overlaying text, etc. could really ruin your eBook. You should consider investing in an eBook programmer, especially if your layout is complex.

Creating a best seller takes time. If you keep cutting corners to rush the process it will be evident in the book. Take your time and patiently develop and improve your book. Go through every process carefully ensuring quality.

Having a book signing at a good bookstore is a big deal for authors. It feels great and in some stores you get to be listed in a newspaper and appear on a local news station. It is important that you try to meet some of these bookstore requirements.

Learn to manage your expectations. You should aim at your book changing at least one life and sales will start flowing once that one life is impacted. Have realistic expectations and be happy for your achievement, however small.

It doesn't matter how great your book is; if you do not market it, it will not sell. People have to know that your book exist for them to buy it.

A good book requires effort and determination. Invest in professionals like an editor and book cover designer, meet all the requirements, manage your expectations and market your book tirelessly. Ensure that you carefully consider the all things listed and you might just publish the next best seller.

Chapter 15
Hybrid Publishing

There has always been a debate on which is better between traditional publishing and self-publishing. But what if you can have them both? The newest trend in publishing is hybrid publishing; a combination of traditional publishing and self-publishing.

This model of publishing is dynamic. Traditional and self-publishing each has its advantages and disadvantages. However, hybrid publishing enables publishers and authors to take elements they like from each model and create a tailored approach to publishing that is beneficial to all the involved parties.

There is no definite way to define hybrid publishing since possible situations vary. But you can say that it is neither traditional publishing or self-publishing—it is any possible combination of the two. This approach can be used for an entire career or just a single project.

AN AUTHOR THAT STARTED his or her writing career by traditionally publishing books decides to venture into self-publishing; the author may end up self-publishing books and traditionally publishing others.

An author who has been self-publishing books may be picked by a traditional publisher.

An author might land a traditional book deal to print a book but still, go on self-publishing ebooks and retain all digital royalties and rights.

A new author is always a risk to any publishing house because there is no guarantee their book will sell. With hybrid publishing, publishers have the option of signing authors who have been self-publishing and already have an audience. The publisher is sure the book will sell to existing fans and readers. The risk is lower and the book has a higher chance of selling multiple units.

Authors earn a higher percentage of royalties when they self-publish, provided they price their books wisely. If a writer prices their book between $2.99 and $9.99 on Amazon Kindle, they get 70%. That is far much better compared to traditional publishing where royalties are 25% for eBooks and 7-10% for a paperback. An author who has been publishing traditionally can take advantage of their existing audience and self-publish several books to enjoy larger royalties.

Publishing a new author's material is a risky process for publishers. They go through the trouble of hiring staff to read book excerpts, full texts and query letters. They have to pay editors to review texts and decide if they are worth publishing. Moreover, they have to pay a team of professionals; cover designers, distributors, printers among others, with no guarantee the book will sell.

Thanks to hybrid publishing, recruiters can go through self-published books online and see the reviews and ratings to determine whether an author is worth signing. It is no longer necessary for publishers to continue catering to the expenses of signing new authors. It also does not make sense for authors to continue with the exhausting process of contacting publishers and agents instead of using that time to market their books and build their career.

Hybrid publishing is the better option for both publishers and authors. Publishers get the benefit of lower risks and authors can earn more from their work.

Chapter 16
A Complete Guide to Ghostwriting

Lately, everyone wants to write a book, and they end up writing regardless of their field of practice. Butchers, snake handlers, candlestick makers, bakers and cake decorators—every amateur and every professional has either written, is writing or means to write a book about their life story, their hobby or their work.

Those who have always known that they were born writers, and have spent their adult life trying to print their books can only stare, surprised as the over eager amateurs pervade the shelves of Amazon.

You should know; those wannabe writers did not write the books! They hired a professional, a ghostwriter.

If you are a businessman and you think a book about you or your business could be a bestseller, but you are not sure if you can write; you need a ghostwriter. Everyone hires a ghostwriter for various reasons. Nowadays, those "authors" you see all over are independent entrepreneurs who utilize books to offer specific business functions like publicity tools, advertising, and calling cards.

Maybe you think that having your name on a book you did not personally write is cheating. Well, a while ago, people would have considered that "telling a lie," but not anymore. Hiring a professional writer is becoming more commonplace and more acceptable. Readers now know that those compelling celebrity bios were not written by the famous names on the covers. This acceptance has extended to other fields as well. People understand that nobody can do it all. A renowned chef cannot discover awesome recipes and write best-selling memoirs at the same time.

Besides, the ghostwriter does not come up with the content; you provide the content by telling them your story in an interview or by writing for them notes, rough drafts and outlines.

Why You Should Hire a Ghostwriter

• Professionalism shows. A professional writer will deliver high-quality work than you, an amateur.

• Time is money. Writing a book is time-consuming. So instead of spending ten hours a day or more writing, a ghostwriter can do it while you work on your business.

• Industry know-how. Experienced writers are knowledgeable when it comes to the publishing industry, and they may also have publishing connections.

• Practice. You have to explain your business in details to the ghost writer. This helps you articulate the bolts and nuts of your product and service consequently building practice for media, public speaking and other PR appearances.

• Team building. If you find a great writer willing to work with you on a long term basis, then that is one more professional on your team.

Why You Should Not Hire a Ghostwriter

• Cost. Hiring a ghostwriter can be expensive. If you have the money, hire one; it is a great investment. If you do not have the money, it is unfortunate. However, you can take a few classes and do it yourself.

• Moral concerns. As pointed out above, hiring a ghostwriter is not cheating. But if you are still bothered, feel free to give credit to the ghostwriter (on the Acknowledgements page).

There is no good reason not to hire a ghostwriter unless it is too expensive for you. You get to have a veteran write your book in a way that you can't. Talk to people who have hired ghostwriters before and those who preferred to write their books. Gather as much information as you can to help you make up your mind.

Chapter 17

Evernote an Essential Tool for Writers

In this information age where there is access to so much content, it is challenging to keep track of information and notepads that we use to write down our ideas and goals. Evernote is compatible with both PCs and mobile devices. It allows you to store information, organize, and access anything, in addition to syncing your content across all the devices you own.

Evernote allows you to jot down your ideas and plans in "notes," organize the notes into "notebooks" and group the notebooks in "stacks." There is no better way to properly organize future blog posts, courses, book chapters, projects and articles. And that is not even the best part; the app does not limit you to text only, you can attach audio clips, images, word documents, web clippings, spreadsheets and much more.

The basic account allows you to upload a maximum of 60MB of content per month and 25MB of notes. The premium account costs $5 per month or $45 per year and allows a maximum of 1GB of content per month and 50MB of notes.

It only took Evernote 15 months or so to attain their first million users, seven months for the second and just four months for the third—that is 8,000 users daily. They finally hit 34 million users in July 2012.

Things keep getting better with Evernote. It has a feature that enables a user to link it to Voice2Note and automatically transcribes your voice note to text. When you get any particular idea or content, just send it to your personal Evernote email address and even specify its destination if you like.

To do this, you need to open your Evernote app or sign in to your Evernote account. Scroll to the bottom or look for the "account info" section/"sync" tab – that is where you will find the designated email address (it is created automatically when you sign up). Ensure that you add the address to your contacts list for easy access.

While sending the email, write the title of your note in the subject line the way you would like it to appear in the account. You can also add the following in the subject line;

• To send the note to a particular notebook, use @ (notebook name).

• To tag the note use # (particular tag).

Evernote could not have come at a better time. With so much content, plans and ideas to write, you will end up using so many notebooks and losing some of them. But now you can contain all your notes in a single app and even categorize them as you like. Get the Evernote app today and organize your life.

Chapter 18
Book Publishers and Subscriptions

Some eBook subscription services like Scribd and Amazon Kindle have become the center of attention with the promise of becoming the "Spotify for eBooks." However, publishers are not being left behind; several niche publishers are now offering discounts to subscribers.

The subscription services by publishers are all part of a bigger plan to get rid of intermediaries in the book industry. For quite some time now, publishers have been enjoying a mutually beneficial relationship with book sellers. Publishers were maximizing revenues generally by selling books via bookstores instead of chasing higher margins selling to readers directly. This was widely accepted because bookshops were like a showroom where readers would discover books. Also, these showrooms were able to reach a bigger audience than the publishers could ever accomplish on their own.

Today, the tables have turned as both publishers and book sellers are struggling to remain relevant. Digital and online book sales have forced more bookstores out of the market. Publishers are trying to compensate for the tight margins and the reduction in physical display room by looking for new sales channels and revenue streams. This does not necessarily imply taking everything down and starting something new; publishers do not have to dig to find a solution. Magazines and journals are already using subscription services, and small publishers have always offered the services since the beginning.

Advantages of Subscriptions To publishers
• Pre-payment for unpublished books stabilizes cash flow.

• Direct sales get a higher margin compared to retail sales even when a subscriber discount is offered.

• Subscription members are often passionate readers who are always spreading the good word about a book.

• Customer databases have so much information and provide more sales data than retailers.

The most common model involves receiving an upfront fee to pre-purchase at a discount price. This model is suitable for smaller publishers who are only able to release few niche publications every year

IT IS NOT MANDATORY for publishers to issue their entire range to the subscribers but there are several ways in which they can break down the subscriptions into smaller packages for the readers. For example, Amazon Kindle offers a subscription package that is apart of a prime membership for $9.99 per month.

The above subscription examples are a few of the many methods that publishers are beginning to reconstruct their revenue models and open new sales channels to cover for the loss of physical bookstores. Subscriptions enable publishers to create a sales connection with the readers and restructure the financial model of the publishing process. This reduces risks for the publisher and consequently, the author regardless of the fact that it is not yet clear how subscription models influence the author/publisher relationship.

Chapter 19

Find Readers That Love Your Work

I f you are expecting some magical ways you will be disappointed. It does not work like that. You can only gain die-hard fans a few at a time and establishing the bond will take time and effort.

Building a relationship takes time. Consistent writing is the best way to find readers and make some of those readers your true fans. It is not what anyone would like to hear but it is a fact. You have to keep working for a long time and never give up. One book is not enough for you to live on and your footprint will be far too small.

With every book you release, your power multiplies. So keep writing more books; each book will keep adding more readers to your fan base.

Word of mouth is a money machine that works even when you are asleep. It may not earn thousands at first but those pennies are valuable too. Ask any avid readers around (and that should include you as an author, you have to be an avid reader) when was the last time they got a book recommendation from a friend. Also, when was the last time an advertisement convinced you (or any other reader) to read a book?

More often than not, people get book recommendations from family and friends. Ensure that your books are worth sharing to get the word out.

Goodreads is like a word of mouth but better, people are diligently looking for awesome titles and reviews. Get an author account and claim your books—they may already have great reviews and top ranking. Even better, add your photo, bio and a link to your blog.

Use Goodreads correctly, do not seem like an illegitimate author by posting spam or salesman. Try talking to readers in small groups or one on one. Remember to be respectful, polite, with an intriguing personality and release great a book after another.

One more thing, the rating scale on Goodreads is different from that on Amazon. A 3-star rating on Amazon is not good but on Goodreads it means something.

AT THIS POINT YOU KNOW there is no quick way to gain followers. They all require commitment. Well, this last method is no different. Should you use Twitter for your business? Sure. But remember using social media is a tactic, not a strategy. And you must never put tactics before strategies.

FOR EXAMPLE, IF YOU are using Twitter, the strategy is to find someone who might be interested in your work. Using automated direct message movers and follow programs is a tactic. Though the tactics may change, the strategies won't.

Finding readers that will love your work is no easy task. You have to work hard, be patient and never give up even when things don't seem to work. Keep writing as many books as you can to cast a wider net, write interesting books so readers can spread a good word, join Goodreads and make use of social networks. Keep going until your dreams turn into reality.

Chapter 20
Kobo Writing Life

Kobo Writing Life was launched in 2012 as the self-publishing branch of Kobo. When authors submit e-books, they are stacked together with titles from renowned publishers. The director of Self-Publishing and Author Relations, Mark Lefebvre, gave a status update to Good e-Reader and revealed some of the exciting deals they have.

A majority of new authors are not knowledgeable about the Kobo ecosystem and they have no idea how Writing Life can benefit them. Mr. Lefebvre gave a highlight of the benefits of the platform to indie authors. "In a nutshell, KWL offers you a place to publish your eBook for free to Kobo's catalog. You keep 70% for any title priced $2.99 or higher. There's no CAP on that 70% which means authors who publish high value box sets of multiple copies of their books, can offer their readers a good deal without having to give up on margin. (Kindle drops the royalties to 35% if you price above $9.99)."

"Also, via Kobo Writing Life, you're not dealing with a faceless corporation. Yes, we have automated tasks and efficiencies so that authors can easily DIY their way all through the publishing process. But if authors need to contact a real human, they can. We've re-launched a new ticketing system that has allowed us to be more efficient than ever before and offer more personalized responses to authors' concerns. We also have a new community and forum where authors can easily find answers to popular questions."

The KWL team does not only aim at helping authors with their publishing but also to inform and educate writers on the business and skill of publishing. They offer free publishing tools and also ensure that authors perceive the economics of business, great practices for authors etc. to accomplish their goals they have partnered with reputable companies to give the best author services for editorial support, cover design, purchasing ISBNs at discounted prices, audio book production among others.

Kobo Writing Life is a great achievement for the company and 550,000 titles have been published over the past six years. 1,000 to 1,500 titles are published every week. Writing Life keeps on getting better and in the last couple of years they have included a pre-order system, a feature for tracking free downloads and author pages. Kobo tries to avoid adding paid services because "of the history of some other companies out there who seem to exist merely to exploit authors and sell things they don't need." KWL is working to being the ultimate trusted service for authors.

KWL is still trying to optimize and iterate their dashboard according to the KWL user feedback they are getting. The company also launched a survey to their most active users to find out what they do not like, what they like, what they would want to see more, and what new things they would find more valuable. The results of the survey enable them to prioritize their 18+ month backlog of upgrades/tasks and updates that they plan to implement. Mr. Lefebvre added they are BETA testing a new print-on-demand feature for US and Canadian authors.

Chapter 21
Choosing the Best eBook Publishing Platform

There are so many digital publishing platforms that authors can use to publish their ebooks. New services are mushrooming to enable self-publishers and publishers to distribute their books all around the world. There are so many options for an author who is contemplating publishing an ebook. Lately, e-books have significantly flooded the market, especially in the US with English as the primary language.

It is safe to say that e-book publishing is the best choice for every self-publisher due to the following reasons;

• EBook publishing is cheaper compared to print publishing.

• EBooks' are less risky due to the low cost of publishing. Self-publishers have no problem taking a chance on them. If the book does not sell much, you will not have wasted a lot of money.

• The digital market is growing very fast with each passing day. The people that read eBooks in the US are almost as many as those that read print books. By 2018, eBook's will be more popular than print books.

What Should You Consider When Choosing The Best Platform For Your Book?

1. Royalty. Whatever platform you choose, you should know that they have to take a cut of the profits. It varies depending on your choice. Do as much research as you can before committing.

2. Pricing. Some publishing services have set price limits. For example, a new author on Amazon cannot offer their book for free and in other cases you are not given any control over the price. This is not necessarily bad but you may not want to be in a situation where you are

not comfortable with the price and there is nothing you can do. Always set a price for your eBook so that you can choose a service that can allow it.

3. File format. Other platforms out there offer file formatting in addition to their publishing services, although many authors prefer to do it by themselves. If you decide to do your formatting, be cautious because it is not easy. You may want to use formatting software like Vellum and Sigil.

4. Exclusivity. A publishing platform may insist on exclusivity, like Amazon's KDP. If you have several books you can have some of them exclusive to Amazon while leaving others available through open publishing.

5. EBook retailers. The top five retailers include: Amazon, iBooks, Apple, Google Play, Nook Press and Kobo. A majority sell all over the world either through their websites or affiliates. Apart from these five, there are so many others that you can choose to work with.

Publishing Your Books Effectively To More Stores and Gaining Global Distribution

Some platforms refer to themselves as ebook aggregators—they stand between an author and a retailer like Amazon. To put it simply, they are companies that accept your book, and converts it into several formats and make it available to multiple distribution channels. Not only do they aggregate and distribute books but they also offer services like cover design, ebook conversion, print-on-demand and editing.

Finding a publishing platform is not difficult but you have to know what you want. Once you have evaluated your preferences, search for the service that best suits your needs.

Chapter 22
Pronoun for Self-Publishing

P ronoun is a self-publishing platform that was acquired by Macmillan in 2016. Recently, they declared new royalty rates for all ebooks sold in Canada and the US. Moreover, they launched Pronoun Author Pages—a feature that will enable Pronoun authors to make customizable web pages for free.

From January 17, authors publishing their books through Pronoun can receive a royalty of about 70% of the list price for all books sold in Canada and the US priced at $9.99 or less, and 65% for the books priced above $9.99. Before this new royalty rate, Pronoun authors only earned 35% for books priced at less than $2.99, just like Amazon's KDP program.

Josh Brody, Pronoun's president said, "We've spent the past year listening carefully to authors and are proud to announce better royalties as part of our continued pursuit of publishing success for writers." Pronoun was launched in 2015 and declared an offer of "a 100% author royalty rate". However, the company has since denied that claim and termed the language "confusing" and noted that "there is a clearer way to communicate benefits".

The head of marketing at Pronoun, Justin Renard, stated that the offer actually meant "no charges on each e-book sale". He added that it is still possible for authors to produce their ebooks through the Pronoun platform for free.

Pronoun offers authors distribution to either one or more of the chief ebook retailers like Apple iBook's, Amazon Kindle, Barnes and Noble Nook, Google Play and Kobo. Books published through Pronoun have to be distributed to Amazon (either by the author or Pronoun), however, Pronoun authors have the option of designating to Pronoun where their books will be sold.

Pronoun lets authors give free books (for example, the first title in a series) and allows pre-ordering for new titles. The Pronoun Author Pages are web pages that are customizable and allows authors to post biographies, photos, and links to their social media accounts and add any other consumer information. The book details are uploaded automatically from the Pronoun book database.

Pronoun was founded initially as Vook; it was an early multimedia technology and e-book platform. It was formed by Brody after procuring several e-book and e-book data collecting companies. Some of the acquired corporations that formed Pronoun include; Booklr (founded by Brody as a data analysis service for ebook sales), Byliner (a literary ebook publisher), and Coliloquy (a platform that uses enhanced apps and ebooks).

While Brody was being interviewed at the PW offices he stated that the company spent six months incorporating into the new parent company. Brody said that the new royalty rates are amongst "the best in the market" and offer "flexibility on pricing and distribution." He depicted the Pronoun Author Pages as "an easy to use tool that allows authors to be professional without being an expert (in web development)."

Brody added that Pronoun obtains revenue from various data analysis and publishing partnerships with companies like The New York Times, Forbes, among others. Nonetheless, he refused to give a specific figure for the users currently using Pronoun.

"We're taking a long term view of the self-publishing market in an effort to attract authors to our platform," said Brody. "We think developing a vibrant user base will provide better opportunities both for us and for our authors."

Chapter 23
Self-Publishing on Amazon

S o many people desire to write a book someday in their lifetime, even though they do not regard themselves as writers. The best time to write that book is now. Self-publishing is no longer stigmatized, and there are numerous success stories of first-time authors who are making a name for themselves. They accomplish this by publishing their ebooks on Amazon.

Forget everything you know about Amazon for a minute. It's not just an online shopping web store or cart. Ask yourself why people like Seth Godin and Guy Kawasaki publish exclusively on Amazon. It is a big deal.

• Amazon is the largest paid search engine globally.

• Amazon has dominated the book industry.

• It's review system is an authority metric even when people plan to buy elsewhere.

• It is a marketing machine when you start selling a given number of copies, it will refer your work to users who do not know about you.

• It is easy. There are only a few sites that can get your book online and published in a matter of hours.

Step 1: Write

The first step to publishing an eBook is to write it, of course. You can do it in three drafts;

• The "Outline Draft". This is self-explanatory in that, you "Outline" on a blank page. Here you write a rough idea of the Table of Contents; outlining every chapter, jotting down your thoughts, stories and scenes. It does not have to be pretty; just make it.

• The Review Draft. Develop your story and how you want to tell it.

• Editorial Draft. Here you have to get a professional editor to help your story structure and style elements.

Step 2: Format and Design

Once you like what you have written, do this;

1. Format your book for Kindle. You can do this for yourself by using Amazon's easy tutorship. Or hire someone.

2. Design your cover. Hire someone.

3. Double check. Get friends to check for errors.

Step 3: Publish

Do not be intimidated, this part is not as scary as most people think. Just sign in to kdp.amazon.com (make sure you have an Amazon account).

Step 4: Promote

Before you start promoting your book, get reviews. Ask friends to leave a review of the book.

Step 5: Launch

Every launch should be unique but some of the tactics that work include sending an email to friends, family and fans, offering incentives to those who will buy the book, marketing on social media and sharing your book with book directories and online forums among others.

Chapter 24

How Should You Price Your EBook

Considering the effort and time you put into writing, editing and designing your book, it is only normal you find it priceless. However, if you are looking to sell your book, you have to price it reasonably. How do you know if the price you have set is too low, too high or just right?

That said, you must come to terms with this one fact;

Selling Your EBook Will Not Make You Rich

Hurtful, but it is the truth. Very few authors have become rich selling e-books. The demand for e-books is on the rise, but the market is extremely saturated, and the prices are quite low, you can barely make a profit.

Kindle Direct Publishing has parameters in place for ebook pricing depending on the size of the e-book. Amazon's parameters can hardly help you price your e-book correctly, and it may end up on the worst-selling list. A wise thing to do would be to ensure that you meet the minimum file size requirements.

The genre is probably the most important factor to consider when pricing your ebook. Is your book poetry, nonfiction, or fiction? Is the sub-genre well known? Make sure to have a look at other e-books in your genre and compare the prices. $2.99 is always a good starting price.

Your book's page count will determine its price. File size may be the primary concern when it comes to Amazon's parameters, but the page count is what tells the buyer how much content they will get. In most cases, books with a page count of 400 and above are always priced higher

($4.99 and above), and those with 400 pages and below are priced lower (below $4.99).

Comparable titles are a great deal. Do a lot of research and find out how authors with similar books have priced them. These books will be your biggest competitors, and you need to price yours competitively. If you go with this advice, you may have to price your ebook lower (or higher) than you expected. But you have to get the price right.

The same way you researched on books identical to yours, now you must study the authors that are similar to you. Research the writers who have a catalog of work like yours (this is easier if you only write for a single genre).

You may notice that your book is not selling yet you have promoted it tirelessly on social media, a fantastic website and other active campaigns—then you should consider lowering your price.

Every time you raise or lower your price, check your competitors' books and ensure that you are within the price range. Pricing your books high may benefit you because of "perceived value" but increasing the price too much will make buyers prefer your competition's work over yours. Make a point of always pricing your books just right.

Chapter 25

Word Count for Your Self-Published Novel

D oes the size matter, if it is a self-published book? Many authors believe the word count is not necessary; as long as you tell your whole story, it doesn't matter whether the book is 30,000 or 300,000 words. However, if you care about marketability, then the answer is not that definite. Be it self-publishing or traditional publishing, chances of success are higher if you hit the word count sweet spot for that particular genre.

Literary Fiction - This genre focuses mostly on themes and issues as opposed to action. These novels range from 40,000 words to 120,000 words. If you are a first-time author with no substantial audience, you should consider sticking to a 70,000 to 100,000 window.

Mainstream Fiction - Also known as "commercial fiction" or "general fiction," mainstream fiction novels have the best odds of success when the word count lies between 70,000 words and 100,000 words.

Young Adult - This genre has very many sub genres, and the protagonists are usually 12-18 years old. Consequently, targeted readers are of that same age. The word count in this genre depends on the particular subgenre, but they should always fall within a 40,000-75,000 word range.

Romance - At the moment, romance is the best selling self-published genre. The general word count for romance novels is between 80,000 and 100,000. However, category romance books (erotica, Harlequin) have stricter guidelines.

Sci-fi/Fantasy - This one is also a top-seller, and the perfect word count is from 80,000 to 150,000. (But supernatural novels often require a higher word count because they create an entire world).

Mystery - These novels are usually shorter since they rely so much on quick pacing. Your mystery novel should never exceed 100,000 words. For "cozy" mysteries, a 75,000-word count is better.

Historical - Historical books mainly cover a particular event or issue—and even give details of an everyday life of the specified period. A beginner should stick to 100,000 words.

Thriller/Horror - You need a strong plot and characters to uphold the suspense. Keep the word count between 80,000 and 120,000 words.

Keep your focus on the right numbers. Do not concentrate so much on the number of pages; the word count is what matters. Take an example of two 300-page books. Though the two may have the same page count, spacing, font size and trimming may hide the fact that the word counts are very different. The word count is what shows the right book length to both readers and publishers.

Use the best font and formatting. When deciding on the font and spacing for your print version remember that readability is important. Your pages should be simple and clean. Get the correct font and paper color that is easy on the eyes.

What is the right trim size? The trim size is the size of a physical book, and it differs based on whether you have chosen paperback or hardcover format, the word count and whether the book is meant for mass marketing. Most publishers have trim size requirements in place, based on the word count.

Each genre has a specific word count which is the same for both self-published books and traditional publishing. This is not entirely limiting—a longer or shorter book can also be a bestseller. The word count is important but so is telling your entire story in the best way.

Chapter 26

Before You Self-Publish a Chapbook, Poetry Book, or Collection of Poems

F inding a publisher for your chapbook, poetry book or collection of poems can be quite challenging. Many famous traditional publishers have no interest in chapbooks or poetry collections. As a result, many poets have decided to take care of the publishing process by self-publishing their poetry manuscripts. If you are one of those poets, it is essential that you do extensive research before you do so.

Your poems may be regarded as previously published work. Literary journals have a small chance of publishing work that has been published before. Try self-publishing a collection that features your poems that have been previously published in literary magazines (include attribution to the literary journals). A strong submission strategy will help you maximize the number of accepted poems.

Do not do it alone. At times, the self-publishing process is frustrating, exhaustive and complicated. Once you have decided to self-publish, you will want to avoid a headache that comes with trying to understand the technicalities of file conversions, formatting or cover art design. Hiring professionals to help and guide you through every step will lift a lot of weight off your shoulders.

Many poets prefer to self-publish their poems as chapbooks (smaller books, usually 25-60 pages suitable for smaller print runs and cheaper to produce). Another great option is to self-publish an e-book instead—it will be easier to edit it later if the need arises.

You should have an online author platform up and running. Distributing your collection calls for hard work. You have to commit a lot of time and effort to building a solid marketing strategy, even before your collection is published and is ready for distribution. Let your social media accounts (more so Facebook and Twitter), and author website is active building a fanbase.

Start getting ready as soon as now so that when your book is out, you can give away free copies as gifts. List your book on Barnes and Noble or Amazon and sell it at your local gift or coffee shops. Book signings and reading arrangements should also be in place.

Selling your poetry collection won't make you rich. Self-publishing is not some get-rich-quick scheme for any genre and especially poetry. Having very high expectations will lead you into greater disappointments or even depression. Manage your expectations.

• Always start with your best poems. The first and second pages will significantly influence a reader's decision to buy your book. Make it count.

• Organize your poems by mood (joyful, despairing, and optimistic) or theme (personal growth, love, nature). You can also arrange them in a manner that will tell a story from the start to the end.

• If a poem does not fit with the overall theme, leave it out. Save it for another collection, however good it is.

• If your poems are visual and meant for children, make sure the font or layout forms an image.

• Your cover should reflect the overall feel of the poetry.

• Proofread again and again. Avoid embarrassing mistakes in your book.

Chapter 27

Getting Book Bloggers to Review Your Book

H aving a fantastic review on your self-published book will give you a sense of pride and satisfaction. But that is not the only advantage of great reviews. Bookstores prefer to have physical copies of greatly reviewed self-published books on their shelves. Moreover, word-of-mouth campaigns are more facilitated by the opinions of online reviewers and book bloggers. If for instance, a popular blogger reviews your book, the five-star review may go viral.

The idea sounds fantastic, and it is, but getting a social media celebrity or blogger to review your book will cost you a lot of effort. Also, you will need a great plan.

Begin by researching and gathering information on book bloggers who may have interest in your topic or genre. Use search engines to search for keywords. Talk to your fellow writers and ask for recommendations of book bloggers. Lastly, spend most of your time on social platforms for book lovers like Goodreads. To find book bloggers on Goodreads that might be interested in reviewing your self-published book, look for a book that is similar to yours and check the reviews (especially the most popular reviews).

Make a point of commenting on your target blogs and request friendship on social media. If all goes well, you might establish a relationship with your target book blogger even before you ask them to review your book. It is not possible to befriend every book blogger who can review your book but do your best to show support for book bloggers.

As you are getting to know your target book bloggers, introduce yourself. Have a template that can be modified and personalized to suit a specific blogger so that it does not look like a forum letter. The letter should always be sincere and friendly, addressing the particular reason for which you contacted the blogger. Include an author bio, your book summary, and contact details. You can even offer a free review copy.

Most online reviewers and book bloggers like to give away copies of books to their fans. Hosting a contest is a great tactic to increase publicity for both the book blogger and the author. Offer to promote your target blogger's contest to either your mailing list or social media followers, and they may decide to review your self-published book.

Create an Excel file to help you track email addresses, dates and responses. You will be able to remember that particular blogger who seemed to like your work so much.

If a potential reviewer goes without contacting you for a few weeks, follow up. Send them a brief note with a polite reminder (with the original text of your initial letter below your signature). Do not follow up publicly, consider keeping the correspondence private.

Note: Not Every Blogger Will Be Interested In Reviewing Your Self-Published Book

Do not terminate the relationship if the blogger turns down your request. They may not want to review your first book, but they may like your second. Always thank the blogger for their consideration.

Chapter 28
Book Trailers

Whether you're self-published book will become a bestseller or not, greatly depends on you standing out among your competition and capturing the attention of potential readers. With so many books in the market, the titles competing for buyers' attention are countless. To rise above the competition, media-savvy authors have discovered the use of book trailers to attract readers and boost their sales.

Most authors do not see the essence of using a video to market written work. But look at it this way; you have seen and most likely experienced how effective movie trailers can be. A great movie preview will entice you into buying a ticket. In that same way, a well-crafted book trailer will engage your audience more and make them interested in your book.

A video advertisement has a stronger appeal. 96% of shoppers confirmed that videos help them when making purchasing decisions and a 92.6% said that visuals are very influential and affect their choices by a great deal. A professional trailer will enable you to engage more of your readers and entice them to click "buy."

A video can reach audiences that you would not otherwise reach. A lot of buying experience nowadays occurs online. You can easily share your book trailer on social media platforms like Twitter, Tumblr, Google+, YouTube and Facebook and allow a potentially infinite audience to have access to your book. Another great place to share your book trailer and generate interest is your Goodreads author page. Also, do not forget to include a link to your advertising video in a mail to your email list as a creative way to engage your fans.

Your potential readers will be captivated. The choice of whether to buy a book or not is made in a few seconds. A short enthralling book trailer with an intriguing teaser will amaze potential readers and make them interested in buying your book.

It should be short and sweet—60 to 75 seconds is just perfect. Now, if a three-hour long movie can be summarized into a two-minute movie trailer, then your book can be summed up into a minute-long preview. The point of the preview is to capture the spirit of your self-published book and leave the viewers screaming for more. It should not reveal every detail of the book and give away the ending.

Do not use your mobile phone to shoot your book trailer. The poor quality will give a bad reflection of your book and turn readers away. If you know very little or nothing about film editing, consider hiring a professional to do a great job for you.

Show potential buyers when your book will be out and where they can get it. You do not need to go into debt just to create a book trailer. An attractive within-the-budget trailer can get the job done.

Chapter 29

Ins And Outs of Copyright

You have religiously followed all the recommended steps before self-publishing, and you have an ISBN, but now you are wondering if you should copyright your book as well.

This is not a legal article, but it will offer you a short overview about copyright and assist you in making the right decision before you make your book available in the market. For more details, you should talk to a lawyer who is an expert in intellectual property and copyright law.

According to the U.S copyright law, your self-published book (or any written work) is protected the minute you put a pen to paper. Copyright is entirely based on your "creative authorship" and does not depend on any formal agreement with a self-publishing company or any book publisher.

Your book is copyrighted as soon as you write it. Now, many people wonder, "how does someone copyright a book?" or "how does someone register a copyrighted book?" The U.S Copyright Office keeps a record of all registered copyrighted materials in the U.S. So, for your book to be listed together with the other millions on file, you have to register it with the office.

Copyright registration guarantees you, a self-published author, more confidence and security in protecting your work. Regardless of the fact that your work is copyrighted the minute you write it, you have to register it to obtain legal protection in a court of law.

As a self-published author, no major publishing house will defend you in a court of law. In the case of someone infringing upon your copyrighted work (or if you are accused of infringing upon theirs) having your book registered with the U.S Copyright Office will help in proving your authorship in front of a judge.

Unfortunately, copyrighting can only protect the text of your book—not the ideas or title. You can choose to copyright your title, but the process is long and tedious.

Why Go Through The Trouble When You Can Just Mail The Book To Yourself?

This method is known as the "poor man's copyright" technique. But unfortunately, you cannot email your self-published work to yourself instead of registering a copyright. You should have official registration.

Does This U.S Copyright Extend Overseas?

The U.S has many agreements with other countries that respect the copyrights of citizens globally. You can Google the list of all countries where your copyright is honored.

Registering your copyright is the right thing to do if you want to shield yourself against potential legal challenges to your authorship. These problems do not occur often, but the risk may outweigh the registration fee. As soon as your book is complete (before you release it to the market), the process of registering your copyright is easy, cheap and may save you a lot of resources in the future. Again, after registering your copyright, the book may be assigned a Library of Congress number.

Do not worry. The U.S Copyright Law provides for such instances. You can always register your copyright up to "five years after the initial publication of your book."

Chapter 30
Facing Critics

Your family, friends, and die-hard fans may be praising your new self-published book—which is great. But what if you introduce it to the general public and you get a bad review? It's okay to feel crushed and frustrated, but have courage; you are not alone. Some of those famous novels you admire have also received bad reviews. It is not possible to please everyone; so do not try to.

Reacting too fast to a negative comment or bad review about your self-published book is a mistake you must never make. Get away from the computer and breathe. Try not to type a quick emotional response. Potential readers are likely to be turned off by a heated argument amidst your book's reviews—they will appreciate a friendly attitude more.

When you see a bad review, you will be tempted to start defending the book, forgetting that every single published book had its share of negative reviews. Give your readers space to form their own opinions, positive or negative—this will prove that you believe in your writing.

Reading a negative comment about your work is never easy, but it will help you grow as a writer. Try to look for constructive advice in a negative review and consider it when you decide to write another book. Honestly, you cannot learn from every single review but learn from those that are constructive criticism. Sometimes, the criticism will be too disheartening; in that case, use affirmations to regain your confidence as a writer.

You may write forty books, and none of them will be perfect. The sooner you accept this fact, the better. Get over that pressure of being perfect and understand that your book is great just as it is—and it cannot be better. This acceptance will help you cope with the bad reviews.

Some of the people leaving negative comments are just being mean. Internet trolls should never stop you from promoting your book or self-publishing again. The best way to respond to a negative comment is to move forward, be better and attain your writing goals. The fear of criticism and negative reviews must never hold you back.

Your colleagues, family, and friends will always be there for you. They will tirelessly attend your readings, offer you a shoulder to lean on, give you advice, and the courage to move on. Never go through the agony alone.

Negative criticism and reviews will always be there. You should always be prepared for them when you make your book available for sale. Remember always to remain calm, avoid getting defensive and learn something from the bad reviews. Perfection does not exist; do not try to chase it. Finally, join a support group to help you cope and do not be afraid to self-publish another book.

Chapter 31
The Art of Kindle Keywords

Kindle keywords are critical when it comes to Amazon eBook sales. Choosing the correct Kindle keywords can create doors for new markets and increase the audience for your book. Keywords help algorithms find your ebook and index your information. The bottom line is, they are crucial, and they must be understood and harnessed.

This chapter will help you differentiate between "Search Engine Optimization Keywords (SEO)" and "Amazon Keywords." You will also learn two secrets to finding money-making keywords and where you should place your keywords to optimize your ranking.

Keywords must be used appropriately, and in using them, you must never do the following;

• Change the purpose or intent of your book for the sake of satisfying keyword searches.

• Intentionally fill your Amazon product page with multiple keywords so that you rank higher.

• Do not try to add keywords that do not even relate to your book.

Keywords are the target or specific phrases or words that you would like your book to rank in search engines' results, such as Amazon.

For example, if you write a sci-fi book entitled "Galactic War Lords," you will want the book to show up whenever someone searches "space war," "space opera," or "military sci-fi." If your book only appears when users type in the exact title, you will have very little traffic.

To increase traffic on Amazon, you must know the most searched phrases and words and which of those phrases and words have little competition.

There are seven key words that Amazon requests from you when you upload a book—those are Amazon keywords. SEO keywords, on the other hand, are universal. They apply to not only Amazon but to other search engines like Yahoo and Google.

The first two (or one) keywords are chosen to grant you a specific category. From there, your Amazon and SEO keywords will be somehow similar. Amazon has a rule that restricts you from selecting an Amazon keyword that is in your book title or any of your book's sales pages. So for your Amazon keywords, consider choosing phrases or words that are synonymous with the SEO keywords.

The art to choosing the perfect keyword is getting the ultimate combination of low competition and high demand. There are two methods of doing this; one is free, slow and not very useful, the second one is paid, fast and very efficient.

Amazon lets you know which keywords are most popular on their site if you follow the following simple steps;

1. Use Amazon Search to See Potential Keywords

2. Check to see how competitive those keywords are—see how many books rank for the keyword, how strong they are and if there is much interest in them.

3. Check other sources for keyword competition.

The other cheap (read paid) method is using KDP Rocket; which is a software that does all of the above for you.

Keywords are essential if you are looking to increase the audience for your book. You have to research, understand them, and know how to use them to unleash their power.

Chapter 32

It's Time to Get a Literary Agent

As a self-publisher, you must act as your own CEO, and for some authors, success in self-publishing can be too much to bear. Many indie writers love to be in control of their destiny, so what benefits can a literary agent add to their career plans?

You are making a significant profit - If the royalties of your self-published book are bringing in money, it is time to find a literary agent who will take advantage of your early success by linking you with a fantastic book deal.

You have had some incredible media attention - If your self-published work has media coverage and reviewer feedback that shows that your book has a substantial audience, leverage your early publicity and partner with a literary agent who will capitalize on the momentum and assist you to unlock many more opportunities in the publishing industry.

You have received inquiries from literary agents and editors - If editors at traditional publishing houses are eyeing your self-published book for potential acquisitions, get yourself a literary agent. A good agent will see hidden opportunities and help you exploit them – even though you might not want to license all your rights to a publisher. If a not-so-famous literary agent shows interest, you can leverage that attention into having a conversation with the literary agent of your choice.

You begin getting requests from subsidiary rights agents - Literary agents who are experts in subsidiary rights are usually more interested in secondary rights like film rights, audio or translation. If requests about your book's secondary rights start coming in, you should hire a dedicated literary agent to negotiate terms with other agents who will approach.

You want to expand your territories - Previously, literary agents presented a writer's entire written work and every form of book publishing. In today's world, they have no problem representing only a portion of an author's empire; which means you can get an agent to represent some rights and leave those that you want to hang on to.

You need help self-publishing - If you are an independent-minded author, you can get an agent willing to act as a partner, managing either all or part the self-publishing process for a commission. This type of literary agent may even help you explore traditional opportunities.

Be cautious; just because you have signed a contract with a literary agent does not guarantee you future success. For some writers, the assistance of a literary agent will benefit their careers, while for other authors, an agent's effectiveness and efforts might just bring disappointments. Before you decide to get a literary agent for your self-published book, weigh the advantages and disadvantages.

While some authors search for the services of a literary agent for positive reasons, others may start querying because the self-publishing process was a disappointment. Physical exhaustion and low sales are among the reasons that push a writer to seek help.

Chapter 33

How to Start a Book Publishing Company

Many self-publishing entrepreneurs wonder how they can create a publishing company at some point in their career. Most of them may not know this but starting your own publishing company will help not only your book sales, but it will also protect you in the process.

Unlike in the past, creating a publishing company is no longer tedious and time-consuming. This chapter will teach you the benefits of a publishing company (LLC) to both you and your books, what you should know before you start the business, and how to start a publishing company online.

In case your services, book, or products get sued, and you do not have a company, your public record and personal finances will be at risk. A company offers you legal protection and assists you to distinguish between your personal finances and the business finances.

Starting a publishing company comes with a lot of tax benefits. Firstly, you can differentiate between your business income and personal income. For example, you bring in an income of $100,000 yearly, and your business also brings in $100,000. If you have no company, you will find yourself in a different tax bracket.

If you have a publishing company, you can set up a second Amazon KDP account—since the terms of service restrict you to one. This second account associated with your business will be registered as a publishing account, which has extra benefits.

You have to choose a business structure before you begin creating your e-book company. The various types of businesses include; Sole Proprietorship, S-Corporations, and Limited Liability Companies among others. For a publisher, Limited Liability Companies (LLC) is the best.

Do not make a hasty decision in choosing your company name. It is advisable that your business name reflect your actual business. Pick several names in case the first one is taken.

Choosing to make your home your business place is a bad mistake. Everyone will know where you live and this includes lawyers and debt collectors. A good alternative would be to rent physical space, set up a virtual office or get a UPS mailbox.

The "setting up" part is very simple—you might want to consider using My New Company or LegalZoom which is a service for creating an LLC. Select an LLC, choose your virtual company and if you like you can designate the service to sign corporate documents for you.

See? Not difficult at all.

Today, you can do whatever you want without much hassle, thanks to the internet. Having your company may attract additional annual costs, but its benefits outweigh those costs by far. Do a lot of research to help you make a decision and become a founder/owner/president of your publishing company today.

Chapter 34
Write a Compelling Author Bio

If you are not a household name, you need an outstanding bio. People who visit your book page need three things to convince them to buy your book; book description, book reviews, and author bio. The author bio tells your audience that you are the kind of person they should be reading, it is where you establish a connection with them and make them believe in you. A great author bio can boost your sales.

You should be able to answer the following questions.

What is your book about? If you are writing a contemporary romance novel, for example, your content and personality in the author bio must be different from that of an author writing about taxes and strategies for business owners.

Who is your target reader? When you were writing the book, what was in your mind? Figure out what your target audience will be looking for in your author bio and write it.

What is the best tone and personality for the author bio? If your book is funny, include that same humor in your bio. Also, you can decide to have the author bio give an insight of the personality of the book.

For every sentence you write, ask yourself if it is relevant to the reader. You should know that no one cares that you always dreamed of being a writer. That you have attained your goal is great but do not include it; unless it is a memoir.

Don't get it twisted; this does not imply that you should write an impersonal author bio— if anything you should strive to connect with your readers. Just make sure whatever you write is relevant to the reader.

You should always go with the third person when writing "About the Author." Writing "she/he" instead of "I" may feel a bit weird but at least it will not come across as boastful when you are mentioning your accomplishments.

Even though it is in the third person, everyone knows you wrote your author bio. State your achievements but do not be a braggart, practice modesty, and humility.

You may have a lot of biographical information that is relevant but not many people will be willing to wade through it all. Write something that can be read in a short time and proceed to buy the book. Aim for 75 to 150 words.

Add your social media information and website to let your readers interact with you and know more about you.

Finally, do not forget to add the author bio to your book page. You can go to Amazon Author Central, select your book and add the bio in "About the Author." Writing an author bio is easy but tricky.

Chapter 35

Give Your Book a Title That Sells

Is the stress of creating a good book title giving you sleepless night? You are not alone. Many authors—even the famous ones—struggle to find a catchy title at one point or another. Your title comes second to your book cover, and it can not only significantly impact your sales, but it will also enhance the book's discoverability on Amazon. In this chapter, you will learn all the secrets of creating a killer title and also see examples of good titles.

What is the secret ingredient? What is that magic formula? Here is a bummer; there is nothing like a magic formula for creating a book title. All authors are not the same; they are in different situations targeting different markets.

Below are some of the factors you should consider as you brainstorm to create a title that sells.

An intriguing title will always draw a reader in. It will build curiosity and motivate them to click on that "buy" button. However, be careful. In the quest of creating intrigue, you may end up making a mistake being too broad and straying away from your genre, causing a lot of confusion.

Examples of intriguing titles include;

• Trust Me I'm Lying: Wait, what?

• Pride, Prejudice and Zombies: you know you didn't expect that last part.

• John Dies at The End: Why are they giving away the ending?

All the above titles make you stop in your tracks because of curiosity.

Renowned authors would not care about their titles being discoverable; their author brands will take care of that. However, if you are not a big name, this is something you have to consider. This is where you apply all the knowledge you have on Kindle keyword generation and research. You should write a title that shows up in search results.

What if someone wrote a romance novel titled "Warborn: Battle for Arrakis"? You get the point. Do not make things complicated by moving from your genre and alienating your readers. Create a genre-specific title, one that rhymes with your book cover.

Your title might be the only book content that someone sees. Does it tell them what your book is about and what they should expect? For fiction authors, this can be a tricky affair, but it is important.

Steps To Coming Up With A Good Book Title

1. Brainstorming Title Ideas. Use common phrases (like The Fault in Our Stars, Till Death Do Us Part), consider one-word titles, use some parts of your story like character names (especially if It's fiction),

2. Name generators. If you are still not sure, try title generators. They can help you think of a title, improve your title or grade your title for you.

3. Add emotional trigger words.

4. Do simple checks to ensure that your title is catchy.

A killer title is a game changer both for your book and you as an author. Ensure that you put a lot of thought in creating one. Be smart and put yourself in a reader's shoes. What title could grab your attention and arouse your curiosity?

Chapter 36
Apple's iBook store

Apple has made creating books for sale easy by incorporating ePub and free tools such as iBooks Author in its online store.

IBook store sells books that have been created using apps like Scrivener and Multi-touch books produced using iBooks Author (free on the Mac App Store). As you decide between Multi-touch and reflowable, remember that you can only open Multi-touch books with OS X Yosemite (or later) or in iBooks on an iPad.

After you have created your book, you have to publish two editions. One will be a sample that your readers can download for free while the other is a complete manuscript. If you decide to go with Scrivener for a different book format, create your sample edition by unchecking almost all of the boxes in the export dialogue export until you have only the sample pages. When you are done, export the sample copy in ePub format. iBooks Author creates both the complete manuscript and the sample for you when you hit "Publish".

APPLE WILL ASK YOU to verify your information so they can pay royalties once the threshold is met. Setting up an account is free (unless you sell a book, then they will deduct 30% from every book you sell). Again if you sign up directly, you will keep the entire 70% to yourself, but if you do it through an aggregator, another cut will be made.

An aggregator acts as a middleman for small publishers. Aggregators receive your book and publish it for you, take care of any administration and tax issues and pass on a fraction of the earnings when they pass a certain threshold.

If you'd rather keep the entire 70% for yourself by selling books directly, you will have to open an account with iTunes Connect, and it requires an Apple ID. You probably have one already for downloading music unless you have used it to sell any media via Apple; then you should open another since you can only use an account for a single media type).

You have to register with the US Tax Service before you can sell your books. When you register, you will get a tax number to enter in the iTunes Connect sign up process.

You are ready to upload your book if they have approved your application. If you have used iBooks Author, you completed the first step when you hit "Publish" on the Toolbar.

For a Multi-touch book, click "Publish" in iBooks Author to compile both the free excerpt and the full book. You will also complete the first step by opening iTunes Producer and creating a new project where you will add the exported ePub file and excerpt.

If your book is approved, it becomes available for sale. You can always track your sales and modify the description and price signing in with your Apple ID—the one associated with your iBook store account.

Chapter 37
Conclusion

Publishing your own eBook has never been a walk in the park, but it has been easier by the availability of services, platforms and tools. With so many options for self-publishers to choose from, authors should be sure to position themselves in such a way to reach a maximum audience.

One of the biggest decisions that a self-publisher has to make is which leading retailers (Barnes & Noble Nook Press, Amazon Kindle Direct Publishing, Apple iBookstore and Kobo) and distributors (Bookbaby, Smashwords, Blurb) they should work with.

Most of these services are non-exclusive which means that a writer will hold on to publishing rights and can edit, modify, or even remove the book whenever they like. An author can use as many of these services simultaneously as they wish. However, Amazon has introduced KDP Select which makes this freedom a bit complicated.

EVEN IF AN AUTHOR KNOWS their completed book is fantastic and friends have reviewed and liked it, it is still advisable to hire a professional to review it. A copy editor would be suitable in checking for any typos and grammatical errors. Nonetheless, a content editor is recommended in case there are errors in the story arc or inconsistencies.

Any writer looking to reach a wider audience should also invest in a professional book cover designer to create a catchy cover. Home-made covers tend to look unprofessionally made, and it may reflect poorly on the author and the book in general.

As an author continues to get final proof for their manuscript, they can begin taking the necessary steps to turn it into an eBook. The text has to be formatted so that it resizes and wraps as users toggle between devices or zoom in, the table of contents should be made clickable in a format that is suitable for every reader. All these can take a few hours for authors who choose to go with DIY. Otherwise, they can hire someone to do it for them.

BEFORE YOU UPLOAD YOUR file, preview each of the file formats on their respective devices (Kobo, Kindle, Nook, etc.). Alternatively, use Kindle Previewer from Amazon and Preview from Nook's Press to preview the files from your desktop—they are both free downloads. From there you can upload your book cover and ebook file. The service will ask you for your basic information like name, address (so that they can easily pay you royalties) and book metadata.

Writing and publishing your book is one thing, marketing and promoting it is another. Since a self-published author does not have the marketing resources of a traditional publishing house, they have to commit a lot of time and money to make people aware of their book.

Promoting a book should begin while the book is still being worked on. A writer should have a professional website, social media accounts and an author mailing list already in place to help them connect with potential readers.

A writer who is looking to keep growing must never get tired. Learning is of particular importance and an author should also be an avid reader, adding to their knowledge while learning new trends and services in the publishing world.

More Titles from This Author

Mastering Drones: A Beginner's Guide to Start Making Money with Drones

The Alkaline Diet CookBook: The Alkaline Meal Plan to Balance your pH, Reduce Body Acid, Lose Weight and Have Amazing Health

How To Make Money With 3D Printing: The New Digital Revolution

33 Strategies of Kama Sutra: Make Her Scream - Last Longer, Come Harder, And Be The Best She's Ever Had

Leading Technology of 2017: And Why You Should Know Them

Mastering Bitcoin: A Beginner's Guide To Start Making Money With Bitcoin

Mastering Apps: A Beginner's Guide To Start Making Money With Apps

Mastering Facebook: A Beginner's Guide to Start Making Money with Facebook

Adult Coloring Book for Stress Relief: Gardens, Mandalas, Flowers, Butterflies, Animals and Owls

Kasani's Organic Baby and Toddler CookBook: Fresh, Homemade Foods for a Healthy Start

Know ThySelf: Secrets To Success In Life & Business

Kasani's Cafe': Simple Recipes for Healthy Living

Don't miss out!

Visit the website below and you can sign up to receive emails whenever Adidas Wilson publishes a new book. There's no charge and no obligation.

https://books2read.com/r/B-A-JYCE-QBZO

BOOKS 2 READ

Connecting independent readers to independent writers.

About the Author

Adidas Wilson was born in Chicago, Illinois, surviving a near death experience driving off a bridge in an 18 wheeler and getting hit by a train. Adidas has dedicated his time and effort to educate, motivate, and inspire people around the world to make positive lifestyle changes. Adidas enrolled at the University of Phoenix graduating with a bachelor's in Healthcare Management. Also studying Health care Informatics - Master Degree program at Lipscomb University. Amazon Best Seller's List and mentioned in Entrepreneur Magazine.

www.ingramcontent.com/pod-product-compliance
Lightning Source LLC
Chambersburg PA
CBHW071243170526
45165CB00003B/1223